The Taste
of Chocolate

All photographs by Natacha Nikouline except page 27 (© M. Viard/Horizon)

English-language edition produced by Cambridge Publishing Management Limited
Translated from the French by Alayne Pullen, European Translations
Project Editor: Diane Teillol
Design: Delphine Delastre
Copyediting: Sandra Stafford
Typesetting: Julie Crane
Proofreading: Jenni Rainford
Color separation: Penez, Lille

Distributed in North America by Rizzoli International Publications, Inc.

Originally published in French as *Le goût du chocolat* (volume II of two-volume set *Chocolat*)
© Flammarion, Paris, 2007

English-language edition *The Taste of Chocolate* (volume II of two-volume set *Chocolate*)
© Flammarion, Paris, 2007

www.editions.flammarion.com

Dépôt Légal: 10/2007

Printed in Malaysia by Tien Wah Press

07 08 09 3 2 1

ISBN-13: 978-2-0803-0055-3

PAULE CUVELIER

President of Maison Debauve & Gallais
With the collaboration of Cathy Selena
Photographs and styling by Natacha Nikouline

The Taste
of Chocolate

Flammarion

THE TASTE OF CHOCOLATE

THE VIRTUES OF CHOCOLATE

THE NUTRITIONAL QUALITIES OF CHOCOLATE

Delicious but high in calories, chocolate is very much an energy food, the exact composition of which varies according to its provenance and method of manufacture. Dark chocolate, for instance, at 515 calories per ¼ lb (100 g), contains many hundreds of different molecules, 60 percent of them in the form of carbohydrates, 30 percent in the form of fats, and 5 percent in the form of proteins. The carbohydrates present in the bean starch and the added sugars are assimilated differently by the body depending on the addition of almonds, hazelnuts, or other grains. The highest proportion of starch is in fact found in the unsweetened cocoa powder. As the addition of sugar is detrimental to the cocoa content, it is preferable to consume chocolate in its "raw state," given that sorbitol-type sweeteners only reduce the energy value by 15 percent. The fats associated with the fiber content give chocolate a glycemic index similar to that of dried vegetables or wholemeal bread. Milk chocolate is slightly higher in calories than dark chocolate at 540 calories per ¼ lb (100 g). Rich in mineral salts (calcium, magnesium, phosphorus, potassium, and sodium), chocolate also contains many vitamins (A, B1, B2, B3, B12, and D), trace elements (iron, copper), and substances with stimulant properties including theobromine, an alkaloid similar to caffeine. Also worth noting is the presence of polyphenols, whose anti-oxidant and anti-coagulant properties make it valuable in the prevention of cardiovascular problems.

Contrary to conventional wisdom, chocolate does not increase cholesterol levels. On the contrary, the presence of phytosterols reduces absorption of cholesterol in the small intestine.

The magnesium content of chocolate makes it a soothing and anti-depressant foodstuff. The 800 different chemicals that make up chocolate include phenylethylamine and tyramine, which act as immediate pleasure transmitters via the central nervous system. In addition to the effect of these chemicals, there is the stimulant effect of theobromine and the soothing effect of serotonin.

Page 6 :
The Royal *with wrappers.*

Left :
Cocoa yes . . . but with as little sugar, cream, and butter as possible!

Moreover, chocolate is a food we associate with pleasure and very often with childhood. Hence the feeling of comfort it brings—the memory of innocent past delights that makes chocolate something to be enjoyed without guilt.

Composition: 4 oz (100 g) chocolate bar

	MILK	DARK
Energy (kcal)	540	515
Proteins (g)	7.5	6
Carbohydrates (g)	56.5	60
Fats (g)	32	30
Cholesterol (mg)	5	1
Iron (mg)	1.5	2.9
Copper (mg)	0.4	0.7
Magnesium (mg)	60	112
Calcium (mg)	200	50
Sodium (mg)	90	15
Potassium (mg)	400	365
Phosphorus (mg)	230	173
Vitamin A (mg)	0.09	0.02
Vitamin B (mg)	0.1	0.07
Vitamin C (mg)	0.35	0.24
Vitamin D (mg)	0.0018	0.0013
Vitamin E (mg)	1.2	2.4
Vitamin PP (mg)	1.1	–
Theobromine (g)	0.2	0.6
Phenylethylanine (mg)	20	–
Caffeine (mg)	–	70
Serotonin (mg)	–	3
Tyramine (mg)	–	2

At the heart of this bar is a true, dry ganache—flavor in its purest form.

CHOCOLATE IN ALL ITS FORMS

The chocolate industry offers a wide range of products in a diverse variety of forms to tempt chocolate lovers. From chocolate bars to luxury chocolates, from snack bars to chocolate spread, not forgetting the delicious breakfast drink, chocolate is available in so many different forms. Enrobing chocolate, coating chocolate, dark, white or milk, filled with liqueur or praline, or flavored with orange, provided that the quality is good, chocolate excels in all these forms.

CHOCOLATE BARS
(34 percent of finished goods production tonnage)
Precisely regulated, the designation differs according to the finished product.

• Dark, fondant, or bitter chocolate bars
This type of bar is produced by blending cocoa, cocoa butter, and sugar. There are three distinct categories depending on the cocoa content: family chocolate, chocolate, and superior quality chocolate.
– Family or cooking chocolate is a low-quality chocolate intended for culinary use. It must contain a minimum of 34 percent cocoa, 18 to 20 percent cocoa butter, and 52 to 65 percent sugar. If no sugar is added to the cocoa paste, the bar will be labeled "unsweetened."
– Chocolate (i.e. eating chocolate) is better quality, with a minimum of 43 percent cocoa paste and 26 percent cocoa butter.

— Dark chocolate known as "bitter" or superior can contain up to 70 percent cocoa, 29 percent sugar, and 1 percent soya lecithin and vanilla. It is dry and intense in the mouth, whereas "fondant" or "superior quality" chocolate has a smoother taste and is more fluid to work with. It can contain 48 percent cocoa paste and 32 percent cocoa butter.

Culinary uses: ice creams, custards, mousses, ganaches, confectionery, and drinking chocolate.

• Milk chocolate bars

These are a blend of cocoa, cocoa butter, sugar, and milk powder (or concentrated whole milk). The chocolate must contain a minimum of 25 percent cocoa paste, 16 percent dried milk, and 26 percent fat.

Culinary uses: decoration, confectionery, ice cream, coatings.

• White chocolate bars

These are made from a blend of cocoa butter, sugar, and flavored milk, but do not contain any cocoa solids. Bars contain a minimum of 20 percent cocoa butter, 14 percent dry dairy product, and 55 percent sugar.

Culinary uses: fruit- and spice-flavored desserts.

• Chocolate bars with added ingredients

These usually contain dried fruits, nuts, or grains— such as almonds, hazelnuts, nougat, puffed rice, raisins, sultanas—or honey, cream, or milk.

• Filled chocolate bars

Whatever the filling—fruit, nougatine, marzipan— the chocolate coating must account for at least 25 percent of the overall weight of the bar.

CHOCOLATE CONFECTIONERY
(30 percent of finished goods production tonnage)

The chocolate confectionery market includes all products made from chocolate and other ingredients in a wide range of individual chocolate forms such as *bouchées, rochers, pastilles, pavés, palets* (discs), as well as various original creations and molded "novelty" shapes.

CHOCOLATE CANDY BARS
(15 percent of finished goods production tonnage)

Chocolate candy bars have been a real revolution in the chocolate industry. They can be filled with praline, caramel, grain or dried fruit, nuts, honey, coconut, or nougat—any of the ingredients used in chocolate confectionery. The chocolate coating must account for at least 28 percent of the overall weight of the bar.

Single-origin chocolate has much to recommend it, but today's blending of high quality cocoas from diverse origins is a modern tribute to single-origin chocolates.

COUVERTURE CHOCOLATE

This is the essential "raw material" for chocolatiers, confectioners, and pastry chefs, and without it there would be no enrobing. There are various types of couverture chocolate.

• Dark couverture

Made from cocoa paste, cocoa butter, and sugar, it must contain 32 percent cocoa butter.

• Milk couverture

Made from sugar, cocoa paste, cocoa butter, and 24 percent fat evaporated milk solids.

• Glace or gloss couverture

With 65 percent cocoa butter, this type of couverture chocolate has a high fat content, which makes it more fluid. It is used to coat popsicles with a fine layer of chocolate.

• Other decorative couvertures

Made from sugar, milk, and cocoa butter to which food colorings have been added, this couverture is used mainly for decoration.

COCOA POWDER
(14.5 percent of finished goods production tonnage)

Cocoa powder is used to prepare chocolate drinks or desserts. It includes the following.

• Pure cocoa

This is made from beans carefully selected for their flavor and aroma. Once dried, roasted, and finely ground, they release the best of their flavor and aroma. The extra-fine powder obtained makes it excellent for use in patisserie and drinks.

• Cocoa with added sugar

This will contain at least 1 oz (32 g) of cocoa for every 3½ oz (100 g) of finished product, depending on the proportions stipulated by regulation.

• Fat-reduced cocoa . . .

. . . with added ingredients such as milk powder, malt, or flour. The powder this produces is consumed in the form of hot or cold instant chocolate drinks.

CHOCOLATE SPREADS
(6.5 percent of finished goods production tonnage)

Spreads are made from a blend of sugar, cocoa powder, and fats, which gives them a clear-cut taste and subtle aroma. They are produced in a variety of different flavors including coconut, vanilla, almond, hazelnut, praline, nougat, and caramel, and in dark, white, or milk chocolate forms.

Truffles dusted in cocoa powder.

CHOCOLATE TRADITIONS AND CUSTOMS ACROSS THE WORLD

Chocolate is enjoying great popularity in all the rich, industrialized countries of the world. New chocolate-tasting circles are forming all the time. The beneficial properties of chocolate are being utilized in new moisturizers and body lotions, just as they were among the Aztecs and Mayans. These days, chocolate has become a major consumer product on an international scale. The United States and Canada are the world's leading consumers of chocolate, while Switzerland is the undisputed leader in Europe. Chocolate is consumed in different ways, depending on the country and culture—old habits die hard. Americans are very keen on milk chocolate with a marked preference for candy bars of various flavors. In northern Europe there is a greater interest in the more nutritional and energy-giving properties of chocolate as a basic foodstuff that has the advantage, among others, of withstanding extreme cold. North Americans and Britons consume chocolate both as an anytime snack and, for example, after a formal dinner, where chocolate with a mint or caramel filling might be preferred. For Italians chocolate is an indulgence readily associated with the pleasures of the senses, consumed in the form of fondant chocolates, chocolate cream drinks (cocoa diluted in a thick syrup, i.e. saturated in sugar and alcohol), *napolitains*—small squares of chocolate served with coffee—and the famous and exceptionally delicious figurines called *nus*. The Spanish use and abuse chocolate in the form of drinks of every kind, thick and sweetened, and also in spreads. Germans prefer to consume their chocolate at any hour of the day as a smooth, creamy, and heavily sweetened drink. Belgians love chocolate in all its forms but have a preference for fondant chocolates with milk, cream, or butter. The Swiss remain the experts at producing white and milk chocolate bars with endless varieties enjoyed all over the world. Australians prefer a spicier chocolate that is not too sweet, and flavored with ginger. The Japanese, whose palate is unaccustomed to salty and sweet flavors, enjoy a pure, dark, slightly bitter chocolate. France is the country that most appreciates dark chocolate, producing a quality acknowledged throughout the world, with consumption peaking at Christmas and Easter.

A chocolate drink made from cocoa powder is all very well, but hot chocolate made from chocolate shavings—that's the real treat for the serious chocolate enthusiast.

GRAND CRU COCOAS

In order to fully appreciate different cocoas, one needs, as with wines, to consider both the main varieties (as with vines) and the provenance (the equivalent of the *terroir*).

The three main types of cocoa tree are the Criollo, the Forastero, and the Trinitario. However, there are others known only to professionals in the cocoa industry, such as the bicolor tree still found in Colombia, an elegant, handsome cocoa tree type found in the Para valley in the heart of the Amazon basin, and a wild cocoa tree type hidden away in the foothills of the Río Negro. Indeed it is difficult to identify and list the different sub-species, as they are the result of countless crosses and hybridizations.

Cocoa provenance is almost infinite as the fine cocoas from the north of South America and Central America are mainly cultivated on small farms, each of which has its own micro-climate and different cultivation techniques.

THE AMERICAS

BRAZIL

At the origin of the world cocoa market, Brazil was the leading world producer up to the nineteenth century. Today it remains Latin America's leading cocoa producer.

Grand cru: Brazil

Qualities: refined, warm, long in the mouth.

Culinary uses: drinks, desserts, and coatings. The high fat content makes it perfect for blending with other fine cocoas.

THE CARIBBEAN

The Trinitario variety is grown on alluvial clay in the tropical heat of the Caribbean islands. The rich scents of these fine cocoas produce a chocolate with an exceptional "nose." Its fruity yet barely sweet smoothness reveals delicate flavors of almonds and roasted coffee.

Grand cru: Caribbean

Qualities: rounded, supple, and fragrant.

Mankind has always been driven to experiment and to challenge; indeed, without this quality the world of fine food would be a poorer place.

Culinary uses: ideal for those who enjoy a rounded, balanced chocolate. Will combine well with coffee and spices, and has a light roast nut aftertaste.

COLOMBIA

Grand cru: Colombia

Qualities: well balanced with a fine, subtle aroma, and a biscuity taste.

Culinary uses: sponge cakes, cream cakes, and ice creams.

CUBA

Cuba is home to a very hardy Criollo variety that produces a fine cocoa of surprising freshness on the palate.

Grand cru: Cuba

Qualities: extreme refinement, power, and persistence of taste; woody aroma.

Culinary uses: ice creams, custards, cream desserts.

ECUADOR

Ecuador is a great cocoa producer. The traditional local variety of cocoa tree is what Ecuadorians proudly call the "Nacional," and produces the "Arriba" cocoa, famed for its floral flavor.

Grand Cru: Ecuador

Qualities: an excellent cocoa with a fine and subtle fragrance, and with aromas of jasmine, orange blossom, and honey. It has a balanced, rounded, fruity taste with a slight acidity, and considerable astringency.

Finest quality dried cocoa beans. **Culinary uses:** ideal for recipes that require a high percentage of cocoa.

ISLAND OF GRENADA

The Criollo and Trinitario varieties grown on Grenada produce beans of surprising fragrance that are both intense yet delicate.

Grand cru: Grenada

Qualities: a smooth, rich aroma, and the taste of flowers and spices.

Culinary uses: desserts, ice creams, and drinks flavored with vanilla, cinnamon, or orange.

ISLAND OF GUANAJA

When Christopher Columbus dropped anchor at the island of Guanaja off the coast of Honduras on July 30, 1502, he little imagined that the name would later be given to a fine, potent chocolate produced by blending the very best cocoa beans: the Criollo bean with its aroma of flowers and fruit, and the Trinitario bean with its typically vigorous bouquet.

Grand cru: Guanaja

Qualities: exceptional power, bitterness, and long in the mouth.

Culinary uses: coatings, chocolate desserts.

SANTO DOMINGO

Grand cru: Hispanola

Qualities: slightly astringent, pureness of aroma with licorice, pepper, and nutmeg notes.

Culinary uses: chocolate cakes, and spice and fruit cakes, mousses, flavored dessert creams, and ice creams.

Grand cru: Tainori

Qualities: aromas of citrus fruit and nuts. Long and fresh in the mouth.

Culinary uses: chocolate cakes and cakes with candied peel, confectionery, and ice cream.

TRINIDAD
Grand cru: Trinidad
Qualities: slightly acrid with a taste of dried, roast grass. Delicate, balanced, and bitter.
Culinary uses: perfect for blending and couverture. Ideal for fruit- and spice-based desserts.

VENEZUELA
The grand cru cocoas of Venezuela, produced from the Criollo variety, are known by two distinguished names—the Chuao, and the Puerto Cabello—and are reputed to be the best and finest cocoas in the world. As the birthplace of cocoa, Venezuela also boasts an infinite variety of other fine cocoas produced by blending the Criollo and Trinitario beans with, for example, the rare aromatic power and truly exceptional bitterness of the Aranguani.
Grand cru: Chuao
Qualities: known as "the Romanée-Conti of chocolates" (after the famous Burgundy wine estate), Chuao is a powerful, warm, rounded, and intense cocoa that is long in the mouth with persistent and tenacious but slightly oily aromas.
Grand cru: Puerto Cabello
Qualities: a less powerful cocoa than Chuao, but very fragrant and noted for the fineness of its aromas.
Grand cru: Caracas
Qualities: a subtle, fragrant, rounded, and balanced cocoa.

Grand cru cocoa beans ready to be shipped to the four corners of the globe.

Culinary uses: all types of chocolate dessert (cakes, mousses, cream desserts, fondants, etc).

WEST INDIES
Grand Cru: Trinidad
Qualities: a cocoa bursting with sunshine, it develops broad, full-bodied, spicy aromas.
Culinary uses: combines perfectly with coffee, hazelnuts, and almonds.

ASIA AND OCEANIA
In 1985, Malaysia became a leading cocoa producer, before being overtaken by Indonesia five years later. While Malaysia is seeking to diversify its crop production, Indonesia is endeavoring to increase cocoa production. As in Latin America, the trend is toward large industrial farms.

INDONESIA
Grand cru: Sumatra
Qualities: a rather acid flavor. Releases very fragrant aromas that are short in the mouth.
Culinary uses: in patisserie, combines very well with dried fruit and nuts, and candied fruits, and is excellent in sweet desserts.
Grand cru: Java
Qualities: caramel, walnut, or cinnamon taste, depending on the plantation. A woody, roasted aroma. Subtly astringent and highly fragrant.
Culinary uses: chocolate fondants, custards, confectionery, and coatings. Milk- and spice-flavored desserts.

MALAYSIA

Grand cru: Malaysia

Qualities: acid flavor, very fragrant.

Culinary uses: because of its high acidity level, this cocoa is used for blending with other fine cocoas or in sweet desserts.

PAPUA NEW GUINEA

This island of tiny plantations cultivated on ideal, volcanic soil produces a cocoa that is very fragrant and woody.

Grand cru: New Guinea

Qualities: aromas of cut grass, leather, and earth. An aggressive cocoa that is nevertheless harmonious and sensual.

Culinary uses: cream desserts, ice creams, and charlottes.

SRI LANKA

Grand cru: Ceylon

Qualities: Ceylon is a full-bodied, rounded, warm cocoa.

Culinary uses: drinks, ganaches, chocolates, and coatings.

AFRICA

CAMEROON

Grand cru: Cameroon

Qualities: powerful yet smooth with a subtle roasted flavor.

A bar of São Tomé and Príncipe. **Culinary uses:** chocolates, truffles, and fine pastries.

GHANA

Grand cru: Ghana

Qualities: intense, robust, strong, and clean.

Culinary uses: chocolate cakes, mousses, and custards.

IVORY COAST

The world's premier cocoa producer, Ivory Coast utilizes its natural resources by developing numerous cocoa bean plantations all over its southeastern tropical forests.

Grand cru: Ivory Coast

Qualities: the lightest of the grand cru cocoas with a very characteristic African fragrance. An intense, robust taste that is clean and strong.

Culinary uses: cream desserts, charlottes, and mousses.

NIGERIA

Grand cru: Nigeria

Qualities: bitter but powerful and fragrant.

Culinary uses: sweet desserts, fruit, and chocolate confectionery.

TANZANIA

Grand cru: Tanzania

Qualities: intense, creamy, strong, and fondant in the mouth. A fruity, banana aroma, powerful, and sun-drenched.

Culinary uses: tarts, chocolate and fruit cakes, custards, and cream desserts.

SÃO TOMÉ AND PRINCIPE

This is country of origin of the wild cocoa tree. The cocoa from the Forastero varieties of São Tomé and Principe produces a dark chocolate with a pronounced, powerful taste that combines wonderfully with delicate fruit and spice flavors.

Grand cru: São Tomé and Principe

Qualities: fruity, spicy aroma, long in the mouth.

Culinary uses: cakes, mousses, cream desserts, and filled confectionery.

THE INDIAN OCEAN

The Criollo and Trinitario varieties grown in the Indian Ocean region produce fine cocoas that are well balanced, full of flavor, strong, and fruity.

MADAGASCAR

Grand cru: Madagascar

Qualities: pale, smooth, and fruity.

Grand cru: Manjari

Qualities: fruity, slightly acidic aroma with red fruit notes. Strong in the mouth.

Culinary uses: ideal for ice creams and fruit-based chocolate desserts. Indian Ocean grand cru cocoas combine excellently with orange peel and all candied fruits.

MAISON FONDÉE EN 1800

PRINCIPE
OLAT DE SÂO-TOMÉ
0% de Cacao

CHOCOLATE TASTING

THE GOLDEN RULES

Like a good wine, chocolate should be tasted in accordance with the pre-established criteria set down by connoisseurs. Of the six hundred molecules that have been identified in chocolate, around fifty play an important role in the process of aroma development. According to the "rules of the art," when tasting chocolate the following criteria should be applied: the appearance of the chocolate, its smell, its texture, how it breaks, its taste, and in particular its mouthfeel, and the flavors released to the palate and nose.

Like the best wines, chocolate should be tasted at room temperature so that the full range of its flavor is released on the tongue and the palate. If you want to compare the aromatic nuances of several different types of chocolate, it is important to clean your mouth with water between each one you taste.

SULPICE DEBAUVE ON CHOCOLATE TASTING

As purveyor to several royal courts and the venue of choice for true connoisseurs, Debauve & Gallais has always made it a point of honor to offer a unique range of dark chocolate whose exceptionally high aromatic cocoa content (72 percent, 85 percent, and as much as 99 percent in many cases) is aimed exclusively at a clientele of chocolate purists. Many aesthetes have endeavored to define the ideal rules for tasting chocolate, so we thought it only appropriate to offer chocolate lovers a few of Sulpice Debauve's thoughts on the matter, found in correspondence dating from the 1830s. They relate to the circumstances, the moment in the day, and the manner in which it is best to taste chocolate.

THE CIRCUMSTANCES: A STATE OF MIND

In the ancient culture of the Aztecs of Mexico, cocoa—*Theobroma*—was the drink of the gods. As with many other distinguished dishes, chocolate must be tasted on a palate unadulterated by any foreign flavor. Tasting should be a moment of contemplation, an opportunity to withdraw oneself from the world outside, to escape from everyday problems, and recapture our true values.
"Above all one should take one's time and make each instant of the tasting a moment of eternity.

The Royal (formerly the Choiseul) with its crested band. This type of packaging was common during the first half of the nineteenth century.

In the quiet, surrounded by those close to you, your mind at peace, allow yourself to be absorbed by the experience of tasting chocolate."

THE MOMENT: AN ACUTENESS OF TASTE

The best time to taste a dark chocolate is between two meals, that is to say at a point sufficiently distant from both the previous meal and the next. Hunger in fact sharpens our perception of cold aromas, whereas the start of the digestive process heightens our perception of warm aromas. It is therefore best only to sample warm aromas—such as ganaches—before we eat and to leave the cold aromas—i.e. the pralines—until later.

"The palate appreciates all aromas equally, providing there is not a pressing sensation of hunger or that the taste buds, having been saturated by a copious meal, remain dulled."

THE TASTING PROCESS: CONTROLLED PLEASURE

Sulpice Debauve's directions for tasting chocolate are very precise:

"Placed on the middle of the tongue, delicately broken by the teeth after a few seconds of controlled delay during which the coating begins to warm up, a chocolate kept in the mouth until the subtle aromas it contains are intimately blended captivates the palate with the full richness of its flavors. This divine juice should then be allowed to slide slowly toward the back of the mouth before being swallowed little by little. The palate will continue to hold the

As a poet once said, the man who never combines his 58 percent or 99 percent cocoa chocolate with fine champagne, sake, whisky, or vodka will never know what it is to make the flavor of cocoa truly sing!

memory of the sensations experienced for many moments more."

KEEPING CHOCOLATE AT ITS BEST

Considered to be fresh products, chocolates must be looked after with care. It is essential to keep them in a dry place with a temperature ideally between 64°F and 68°F (18°C and 20°C). Do not keep chocolates in a refrigerator or in a warm room, and try to avoid any sudden changes of temperature. In the case of homemade chocolates, as your technique for preparing and applying the coating chocolate is bound to be flawed, at least during your first attempts, your chocolates are likely to turn white very quickly. This change of appearance, for instance a loss of glossiness or a "cottony" appearance on the surface of your chocolates, is the result of the cocoa butter and cocoa paste separating. Don't worry, this doesn't affect the flavor or mouth quality of your chocolates at all. When you buy commercially produced chocolates you can keep them for as much as a year if you leave them in their original, unopened packaging, and keep them away from humidity and light, and at the correct temperature.

CHOCOLATE AND ALCOHOL

CHOCOLATE AND WINE

The density and bitterness of cocoa does not combine well with heavily fermented wines. It is better to accompany it with naturally sweet wines and liqueurs with an alcohol content of between 15 and 21 percent.

Suitable wines: all naturally sweet wines produced by extended aging and wines with an aroma that complements the bitterness of the chocolate such as a grand cru Banyuls wine, Maury Rancio, Rasteau, and Rivesaltes. The next consideration in choosing a wine is the flavor of the filling, which needs to combine subtly and well with the aroma of the wine. In the case of a chocolate with a praline filling or a full-bodied, dark, fondant chocolate you could try a yellow Jura wine. With a dark chocolate and caramel or salted butter ganache, a Hungarian Tokay would go well, while sherry is excellent with chocolates with a marzipan filling. A Jurançon wine is an excellent accompaniment to chocolates filled with praline or spiced ganache.

Fortified wines such as port (of the oxidative aged type) give off aromas of praline and peanut that combine perfectly with chocolate desserts.
Recommendation: Vintage Tawny port, Colheita port.

Non-French wines can also be tried, such as Málaga wines from Spain or the wines of southern Italy such as Primitivo di Manduria, the great Marsalas, and Vergine Stravecchio, whose aromatic power is produced by ten years of aging. Greek wines such as the Mavrodafni of Cephalonia or Patras have an aroma of coffee, chocolate, and fig that combines admirably with chocolate.

PANCAKES WITH FRUIT AND BANYULS WINE, TOPPED WITH A CHOCOLATE SAUCE

Serves 6
Preparation: 10 minutes
Marinate for: 1 hour
Cooking time: 5 minutes

Ingredients: 1 lb 2 oz (500 g) of strawberries, 1 glass of Banyuls wine, ¼ lb (100 g) of fondant chocolate (between 70 and 85 percent cocoa), ½ cup (10 cl) of crème fraîche, 12 pancakes

Wash and dry the strawberries then marinate them in the Banyuls wine for an hour. Melt the chocolate in a bain-marie. Once it is smooth and runny, stir in the crème fraîche. Fold the pancakes in four and place a few of the drained strawberries between the two folds. Top with chocolate sauce.

Serving tip: eat warm with a glass of Banyuls wine.

CHOCOLATE AND SPIRITS
Spirits combine well with chocolate providing they are not too sweet, too bitter, or too acidic. If using whisky, select one that is robust but not too alcoholic, low in tannins, and not too peaty or iodized. A bourbon with a toasted, honey aroma will combine well with a sweet chocolate, while a Spreyside, sherry cask, or eighteen year-old Macallan will go perfectly with a praline or hazelnut chocolate. A full, filled, semi-sweet chocolate will

combine splendidly with armagnac or an old cognac thanks to their roundness in the mouth. An old rum will be sublime with ganaches and praline fillings.

CHOCOLATE AND HAZELNUT CAKE WITH KIRSCH

Serves 6
Preparation: 25 minutes
Cooking time: 50 minutes

Ingredients: *1 stick (100 g) of butter, 1 scant cup (200 g) of sugar, 3 eggs, pinch of salt, 2¼ tbsp of cocoa powder, 1 oz (30 g) of dark chocolate (78 percent cocoa), ¾ cup (150 g) of flour, ½ cup (10 cl) of milk, 2¼ tbsp of kirsch, 1 cup (150 g) of chopped hazelnuts, 1 envelope of vanilla sugar*

Preheat the oven to 320°F (160°C; mark 5/6). Beat the softened butter with the sugar. Add the egg yolks, salt, cocoa powder, dark chocolate melted in the bain-marie, flour, and milk. Blend together well for 15 minutes, adding the kirsch to the mixture. Then add the hazelnuts, vanilla sugar, and stiffly beaten egg whites. Pour into a greased cake tin and bake for approximately 45 minutes.

Serving tip: warm some red fruit jelly or citrus marmalade in a small pan and spread on the cake.

MILK CHOCOLATE MOUSSE WITH GRIOTTINE CHERRIES

Serves 4
Preparation: 20 minutes
Cooking time: 5 minutes
Refrigeration: 3 hours

Ingredients: *½ lb (200 g) of milk chocolate, 2 tbsp of water, 4 eggs, 2¼ tbsp of rum, pinch of salt, around twenty Griottine cherries (these can be bought in jars, steeped in liqueur and rum)*

Break the milk chocolate into pieces and melt in a bain-marie with 2 tbsp of water. Separate the whites and yolks of the eggs. Once the chocolate has melted, remove from the heat. Then add the rum and egg yolks. Beat the egg whites with a pinch of salt until stiff peaks form, then fold carefully into the chocolate mixture. Stone the Griottine cherries and add them to the mousse mixture. Place in the refrigerator for at least 3 hours. Decorate with Griottine cherries before serving.

GRAND MARNIER CAKE

Serves 6
Preparation: 20 minutes
Cooking time: 55 minutes

Ingredients: *5 oz (150 g) of dark chocolate (70 percent cocoa), ½ stick (75 g) of butter (plus some to grease the baking tin), 4 eggs, ¾ cup (150 g) of caster sugar, ½ cup (100 g) of flour, 1 tbsp of Grand Marnier*

Break the chocolate into small pieces and melt with the butter over a very low heat, stirring occasionally. Leave to cool. In a bowl, beat the egg yolks with the sugar then carefully fold in the flour with a spatula. The mixture should not be too stiff. Beat the egg whites until stiff and add them to the mixture. Then add the Grand Marnier. Pour the mixture into a well-greased cake tin and bake in the oven at 285°F (140°C; mark 4/5) for 50 minutes.

CHOCOLATE AND RUM SPONGE CAKE

Serves 6
Preparation: 25 minutes
Cooking time: 45 minutes
Refrigeration: 2 hours

Ingredients: *1 egg, ¼ cup (60 g) of sugar, ½ cup (50 g) of flour, 3 tbsp of milk, ½ envelope of baking powder, butter to grease the baking tin.*
For the topping: *6 oz (175 g) of dark chocolate (72 percent cocoa), just under 1 stick (80 g) of butter, rum to taste*

In a bowl mix the whole egg with the sugar, flour, and milk. Add the baking powder. Grease a baking tin with butter and carefully pour in the mixture. Bake at 355°F (180°C; mark 6) for 20 minutes. Turn out of the tin and leave to cool on a rack. Over a very low heat, melt 4 oz (125 g) of chocolate broken into small pieces with the butter.
Dribble the cake with rum and finish with this chocolate topping. Grate the remaining 2 oz (50 g) of chocolate, and sprinkle on top. Leave to rest in the refrigerator for 2 hours.

CHOCOLATE AND FRUIT

Chocolate combines especially well with fruit, whether fresh, dried, or candied. When making brownies or muffins you can try new combinations by adding pistachios, hazelnuts, pine nuts, or sliced almonds. You could experiment with making chocolate discs using a fine Cuba chocolate and flavoring them with grapefruit, clementines, lychees, or even mango. And why not try a white chocolate mousse with olive oil on a coulis of passion fruit, or combine a dark chocolate ganache with raspberries or candied chestnuts? Or more daring still, a chocolate fondue with a platter of fresh, seasonal fruit or a bitter chocolate charlotte studded with raspberries, redcurrants, and wild strawberries. A chocolate cake with orange or lemon zest is delicious, unless of course you have a weak spot for the traditional Black Forest gateau! Nature has provided so many options that the opportunities for creating recipes that combine fruit and chocolate are virtually limitless. So make the most of them!

CHOCOLATE FRUIT FONDUE

Serves 6
Preparation: 20 minutes
Cooking time: 10 minutes

Ingredients: *3 tbsp (40 cl) of cream, 1 lb 2 oz (500 g) of dark chocolate (85 percent cocoa), 2 tbsp of brandy, assorted fruit: bananas, pears, pineapple, oranges, lemons, dried fruit such as apricot or prunes, sweet cookies*

Heat the cream in a fondue dish. Add the chocolate broken into small pieces and melt for 10 minutes while stirring. Add the brandy. Cut the fruit into pieces or quarters. Sprinkle the pear and banana with lemon juice. Push the fruit onto wooden skewers and dip into the warm chocolate. Serve with little cakes or cookies.

Serving tip: enjoy with a Maury or Banyuls wine or a semi-sec champagne.

WALNUT BROWNIES

Serves 8
Preparation: 25 minutes
Cooking time: 35 minutes

Ingredients: *½ lb (200 g) of dark chocolate (85 percent cocoa), 1 stick (125 g) of butter (plus some to grease the baking tin), ½ cup (100 g) of caster sugar, ½ cup (50 g) of flour (plus some to dust the tin), 4 eggs, 1 scant cup (100 g) of shelled walnuts*

Preheat the oven to 300°F (150°C; mark 5). Melt the chocolate with the butter in a pan over a low heat. Add the sugar, flour, eggs, and finely chopped walnuts. Pour the mixture into a greased tin dusted with flour. Bake for 30 minutes.

CHOCOLATE AND ALMOND CAKE

Serves 6
Preparation: 30 minutes
Cooking time: 45 minutes
Refridgeration: 3 hours

Ingredients: *9 oz (250 g) of dark chocolate (70 percent cocoa), 2 sticks (200 g) of butter (plus some to grease the baking tin), ½ cup (150 g) of sugar, 3 tbsp of cornstarch, 1 scant cup (100 g) of finely ground almonds, 1 envelope of vanilla sugar, ½ tsp of baking powder, 6 eggs, pinch of salt*
For the topping: *2 oz (50 g) of chocolate, 2 tbsp of milk*

Preheat the oven to 390°F (200°C; mark 6/7) for 10 minutes. Break the chocolate into pieces and melt with the butter in a small pan over a very low heat, until the mixture is smooth. Leave to cool. Then whisk in the sugar until thoroughly blended. In a bowl, mix together the cornstarch, the ground almonds, vanilla sugar, and baking powder. Next add the chocolate and sugar mixture. Separate the whites and yolks of the eggs. Add the yolks to the mixture you have already prepared, and whisk the egg whites with a pinch of salt until firm peaks form. Take a quarter of the beaten egg white and incorporate it quickly into the mixture to aerate it, and then carefully fold in the rest of the whites. Grease a deep baking tin and pour in the mixture. Bake in the oven for 45 minutes. Once the cake is cool, melt the chocolate with the milk in a saucepan and spread smoothly over the top of the cake with a spoon. Leave to cool in the refrigerator for a few hours before serving.

CHOCOLATE AND PRALINE TART

Serves 6
Preparation: 30 minutes
Cooking time: 45 minutes

Ingredients: *¼ lb (100 g) of bitter chocolate (65 percent cocoa), 1 pint (½ liter) of crème fraîche, ½ cup (125 g) of caster sugar, 5 eggs, ½ lb (200 g) of crushed pralines, 6 whole pralines*
For the shortbread pastry: *5 oz (150 g) of flour, ½ stick (75 g) of butter, ½ cup (100 g) of sugar, pinch of salt, ⅓ of an envelope of baking powder, 1 egg*

On a pastry board mix the chilled butter cut into small pieces with the flour, using your fingertips until you have a mixture resembling fine breadcrumbs. Work quickly, keeping your hands cool so that the butter does not melt. Add the sugar, salt, and baking powder, and mix together. Make a hole in the middle of the dry mixture and add the egg. Mix well, and knead until smooth and thoroughly blended. Roll into a ball and leave to rest for at least 1 hour before using. Line a baking tin with the pastry and prick lightly with a fork. Cover in aluminum foil and "blind bake" for approximately 15 minutes at 390°F (200°C; mark 6/7). Remove the aluminum foil 5 minutes before the end of the cooking period. Melt the chocolate in a bain-marie. In a bowl mix together the crème fraîche, sugar, eggs, crushed pralines, and chocolate. Pour the mixture onto the pastry. Bake at 320°F (160°C; mark 5/6) for 30 minutes. Leave to cool, and decorate with the whole pralines.

CHOCOLATE AND ALMOND COOKIES

Serves 6
Preparation: 30 minutes
Cooking time: 30 minutes

Ingredients: *1 cup (175 g) of blanched almonds, ½ lb (200 g) of dark chocolate (70 percent cocoa), ¾ cup (175 g) of caster sugar, 1 egg*

Crush the almonds and grate the chocolate. In a bowl, mix together the grated chocolate, sugar, almonds, and whole egg until smooth and well blended. Spread the mixture out with a rolling pin to no more than ¼ in. (5 mm) thick. Cut into cookies with a small cookie cutter. Place on a baking tray and bake in the oven at 355°F (180°C; mark 6) for 30 minutes.

CHOCOLATE AND SPICES

Originally cocoa was considered to be a spice and certain other spices such as vanilla, pepper, cinnamon, and nutmeg soon became associated with the chocolate drink that revolutionized the taste buds of the courts of France and Europe. The spice tradition is one that chocolate makers all over the world continue to uphold, endlessly seeking new ways of combining spices with the full-bodied flavor of chocolate. Who could forget that wonderful cinnamon-flavored hot chocolate drink that warms us up on long, cold winter evenings?

CINNAMON HOT CHOCOLATE

Serves 2
Preparation: 5 minutes
Cooking time: 5 minutes

Ingredients: *scant 2 cups (40 cl) of milk, ½ vanilla pod, ½ cinnamon stick, 2 tbsp of honey, ¼ lb (100 g) of dark chocolate (85 percent cocoa) broken into pieces*

Bring the milk to the boil with the vanilla, cinnamon, and honey. Add the chocolate and stir well over a low heat for about 5 minutes until smooth and well blended. Serve immediately.

Serving tip: as a finishing touch you could top your chocolate with Chantilly cream sprinkled with dark chocolate flakes.

Serves 6
Preparation: 25 minutes
Cooking time: 1 hour 5 minutes

Ingredients: *½ cup (125 g) of sugar, 3 eggs, ½ lb (200 g) of dark, bitter chocolate (65 percent cocoa), 1 stick (150 g) of butter, 2 cups (250 g) of flour, 1 envelope of baking powder, 1 level tsp of ground coriander, 1 tsp of ground cinnamon, 1 tsp of ground ginger, 2 ground cloves*

Preheat the oven to 355°F (180°C; mark 6). In a bowl mix together the sugar and eggs until smooth and pale. Break the chocolate into small pieces and melt over a very low heat with the butter. Leave to cool, then combine with the sugar and eggs. Put the mixture into a blender. Blend until light and creamy. Add the flour, baking powder, and spices. Blend well again until smooth. Pour the mixture into a greased cake tin and bake at 355°F (180°C; mark 6) for 1 hour.

CHOCOLATE AND CHEESE
Many great chefs have taken inspiration from the surprising yet refined combination of chocolate and cheese, to create new dishes. From spiced canapés and nibbles to novel desserts, it is a combination attracting many new followers fascinated by the originality and disconcerting flavors it produces. A must for anyone in search of new "sweet and salt" sensations.

CHOCOLATE AND CHEESE APPETIZERS

Cut out squares of assorted breads: white, walnut, rye, wheat, and granary. Melt ¼ lb (100 g) of dark chocolate in a bain-marie. Leave to cool slightly and spread onto the squares of bread. Cut cubes of the following cheeses: Roquefort, Comté, Époisses, and Camembert. Place a cube on each bread square. Enjoy!

DARK CHOCOLATE MOUSSE WITH GOAT CHEESE

Serves 6
Preparation: 30 minutes
Cooking time: 5 minutes

Ingredients: *9 oz (250 g) of dark chocolate (70 percent cocoa), scant 2 cups (40 cl) of light cream (15 percent fat), ¼ lb (100 g) of fresh goat cheese, 1 gelatin sheet, 3 egg whites, 1 envelope of vanilla sugar, ¾ oz (20 g) of chocolate flakes, 1 oz (25 g) of pistachios, 1 bunch of radishes*

Melt the chocolate in a bain-marie. Heat half the cream in a small pan over a gentle heat, adding the melted chocolate and goat cheese. Blend until smooth. Dip the gelatin sheet in a little cold water, drain well, and add to the warm mixture. Away from the heat, put the mixture in a bowl standing on ice and mix together. Pour the remaining cream into another bowl and whisk vigorously. In a large bowl beat the egg whites with the vanilla sugar until stiff. Gradually fold the whipped cream and beaten egg whites into the chocolate mixture. Mix together until light and airy. Add the chocolate flakes and ground pistachios, and garnish with radish slices.

CHOCOLATE IN ITS MANY VARIETIES

Before donning the apron of a chocolatier it is worth mastering a few basic concepts.

FILLINGS: GANACHE, PRALINE, AND OTHERS

GANACHE: HALF CHOCOLATE, HALF CREAM

Ganache is certainly the most commonly used filling. If, as often happens, it is too fatty and heavy rather than light, it is because butter has been used instead of double cream. It is our view that the qualities of cream make it preferable to butter. That said, a simple chocolate ganache, when well executed, opens up horizons to explore that are as limitless as your imagination.

One of the greatest delights for the chocolatier is incorporating any of a range of flavors to suit his or her particular taste: spices (in finely ground powder form or after infusing for several minutes in cream); tea or coffee (also infused for several minutes in cream then passed through a fine strainer); fruit pulp and alcohol (added when the chocolate is fully melted)—always in small quantities or else the ganache can lose its homogeneity and become difficult to work.

The length of the infusion time and the quantity of flavoring used are entirely a matter of personal taste. However, in the case of spices, tea, and coffee, one or two small teaspoons should suffice if infused for around five to ten minutes. With alcohol, allow at least six to seven tablespoons (10 cl). Where it comes to making ganache, take a gradual and careful approach: have a trial run following our directions then adjust according to your personal taste.

A ganache is a fusion of 50 percent couverture chocolate and 50 percent cream. It is possible to reduce the proportion of cream by substituting butter, but the weight of the butter must not exceed 15 percent of the overall weight. Choose a good quality couverture because the better the couverture, the better the ganache will be.

Chocolate shavings—the ultimate ingredient for making drinking chocolate.

GANACHE FILLING

Ingredients: 1 cup (25 cl) of heavy cream (or ½ stick (75 g) of butter), 9 oz (250 g) bar of dark chocolate

Bring the heavy cream (or butter) to the boil (1). Remove from the heat. Then gradually stir in the chocolate (broken into small pieces) until thoroughly blended (2). Stir with a whisk or wooden spatula until the mixture is smooth (3, 4). A pinch of vanilla powder is always a welcome addition to a plain ganache. Leave the ganache to stand in a cool place (60°F to 65°F; 15°C to 18°C) for at least 4 hours until it sets. It should be quite firm (5) and must then be worked with a spatula over a gentle heat. If you can wait until the following day, particularly in the case of flavored ganache, the aroma of the spices and alcohol you have added will be all the better for it. 1 lb (500 g) of ganache is sufficient to make around 70 units (i.e. approximately ¼ oz (8 g) each; any smaller would be difficult for a beginner to enrobe with the chocolate). Divide the ganache into pieces and keep in a cool place so that they stay firm. Hand-rolled balls are the easiest shape to coat but as you become more adept you can let your imagination be your guide!

Tip: if your hands are too warm and the ganache "sticks" when you roll it, dust your hands regularly with icing sugar.

1

2

3

4

5

PRALINE: A MATTER OF FINE TOUCH

While a ganache can be produced with relative ease in the home kitchen, a praline filling demands greater skill and a more certain touch. But nothing ventured, nothing gained!

PRALINE FILLING

A good praline mix consists of 50 percent sugar and 50 percent nut (almonds, hazelnuts, or a mixture of the two—we prefer 1 1/3 cup (150 g) of blanched almonds to 1 scant cup (100 g) of hazelnuts).

Ingredients: *1 1/3 cup (150 g) of blanched almonds, 1 scant cup (100 g) of hazelnuts, 1 cup (250 g) of cane sugar, 5 oz (150 g) of couverture chocolate (see recipe page 61)*

Lightly toast the almonds and hazelnuts on a baking tray at 480°F (250°C; mark 8/9). First time round aim to achieve a light brown color. Moisten the sugar and cook it in a pan over a low heat stirring all the time. When it begins to take color remove from the heat and add the nuts. Pour the mixture in a thin layer onto a lightly oiled, cold baking tray. When the mixture has set, break it into small pieces and crush it or place briefly in a food processor until it reaches the desired consistency (fine or coarse as you prefer). Return to a low heat. When the mixture has reached a constant temperature (the grinding process can cause it to heat slightly) add the couverture chocolate, stirring gently with a spatula until the mixture is thoroughly blended.

Producing successful pralines is a matter of fine dexterity.

Once the praline mix has been left to rest it will be sufficiently firm to be divided into about 70 pieces in whatever shape you like. As with ganache, for beginners, praline balls are the easiest shape to enrobe with chocolate.

OTHER FILLINGS

Although ganache and praline are the main fillings used, they are not the only ones. If, for instance, you are fond of nougat, you could try cutting it into very small cubes and dipping these in coating chocolate. The same is true of caramel toffees, *gianduia* (a fine hazelnut paste), marzipan, and other sweetmeats. However, this will not be possible with "softer" fillings, which require the use of molds.

*The stages of a good
couverture.*

1

2

3

4

ENROBING: MATERIALS, COUVERTURE, AND EXPERTISE

COUVERTURE: A MATTER OF BLENDING

Couverture is the name commonly given to chocolate used in the manufacture of chocolate candies, for enrobing, and for the preparation of ganache and praline fillings. You are advised to use a chocolate containing 72 percent cocoa as it requires considerable experience to work chocolate with a lower sugar content, such as 85 percent cocoa. Always be sure to allow double the volume you need—whether making ganache, praline, or enrobing—as this will make working it easier. You will find the chocolate you need to make couverture available in 3½ oz (100 gram) bars. Choose a good blended chocolate rather than one of the "origin chocolates" that have recently become fashionable, as they have the disadvantage of being rather unbalanced because they are usually manufactured without any prior blending trials.

COUVERTURE CHOCOLATE

Ingredients: *dark chocolate (at least 72 percent cocoa)*

Break the chocolate into small pieces. Place three-quarters of these pieces in a round-bottomed metal bowl. Heat in a low oven (120°F to 140°F; 50°C to 60°C). Watch carefully, and stir slowly and often with a spatula. The temperature of the mixture should not be allowed to rise above 104°F or 106°F (40°C or 41°C). You can test for this with the back of your finger. However, beginners are strongly recommended to use a cooking thermometer, as success depends very largely on getting the temperature right.

Once the mixture has reached this temperature, mix in the remaining quarter of the chocolate. Stir until smooth and glossy. This is the "couverture," or coating chocolate, that you will use to coat your candies or make your praline mix. If the mixture is too thick, return it to a very low heat—this time the mixture should not go above 99°F (37°C).

Tip: the temperature of the couverture must remain constant and uniform. It is therefore best to reheat it regularly and stir it constantly. When you have finished using it, leave it to cool; it can be broken into small pieces and used again when you want.

ENROBING: A LONG LEARNING PROCESS

The enrobing process is not, in itself, complicated. It is a matter of producing a couverture chocolate at the right temperature and acquiring the skill to handle it. The more awkward one is, the longer it will take to enrobe successfully, and the more time one will need to spend reheating the chocolate!

This is why we advise starting out by making ball shapes which can be dipped one by one in the coating chocolate and removed with a chocolate fork (or ordinary fork), then placed carefully on greaseproof paper until cool.

When you are more comfortable with the process, you can try the flat shapes usually known as *palets*, or disks. You can also try tracing decorative shapes in the chocolate, covering the disk as it begins to set, using a chocolate fork. If you are keen on chocolate truffles, pour some cocoa powder into a small heap and place the ganache balls into this immediately after enrobing. You can roll them gently in the powder with a chocolate fork to ensure they are evenly coated with cocoa.

Tip: when the coating chocolate is dry, gently toss the truffles in a sieve or strainer to remove any excess cocoa powder.

THE CHOCOLATE MAKER'S TOOLS OF THE TRADE

Although making chocolates does not require an extensive amount of equipment, you will nevertheless need access to a traditional oven, a gas hob, and a few other pieces of equipment that will help to transform you into a chocolatier—albeit a novice one!

— Round-bottomed metal bowl
— 2 wooden spatulas
— Very fine gauge strainer
— Cooking thermometer, which can be dipped in the melted chocolate to check the temperature
— Whisks

— Scraper: a flexible, plastic scraper that matches the curve of the round-bottomed bowl, allowing you to remove all the ganache, praline, or chocolate
— Triangular scraper: a metal, triangular tool for scraping the work surface clean
— Chocolate forks: small forks specially designed for dipping candies in chocolate coating and for decorating them.

RECIPES FOR HOMEMADE CHOCOLATES

The thirteen recipes that follow have been simplified to make them easier for would-be chocolatiers to execute successfully. We felt that the important thing was to focus on the perception of taste. As far as the right chocolate to use for the couverture is concerned, it is best to experiment with some of the different types of "origin" and "blended" bars available. We recommend a minimum of 72 percent cocoa, but would advise against anything over 85 percent, as chocolate with a very high cocoa content is much more difficult to work with.

Scrumptious truffles . . .

DEBAUVE & GALLAIS PALETS

Makes 70

For the ganache: *½ cup (150 g) of heavy cream, 1 stick (100 g) of butter, 9 oz (250 g) of chocolate (at least 72 percent cocoa), pinch of vanilla powder*
For the coating: *2 lb (1 kg) of couverture chocolate (see recipe on page 61)*

Bring the heavy cream to the boil with the butter. Remove from the heat. Slowly add the chocolate, broken into small pieces. Stir with a whisk until the mixture is smooth. Add the pinch of vanilla powder. Leave the ganache to stand in a cool place (60°F to 65°F; 15°C to 18°C) for at least 4 hours until it sets. Divide into about 70 pieces with a round cutter or into balls, if easier. Keep in a cool place so that they become firm. Prepare the couverture chocolate (see recipe on page 61). Dip the ganache balls in the couverture chocolate one at time. Then remove them with a chocolate fork (an ordinary fork will do). Place carefully on greaseproof paper and leave until cold. If you have decided to make disks (*palets*), trace decorative shapes in the coating with a chocolate fork as it begins to set.

Earl Grey palet.
A story that dates back
to the history of Manaus!
Rediscover this taste
of the past.

EARL GREY PALETS

Makes 70

For the ganache: *1 cup (250 g) of heavy cream, 1 to 2 tsp (5 or 10 g) (according to taste) of Earl Grey tea, 9 oz (250 g) of chocolate (at least 72 percent cocoa), pinch of vanilla powder*
For the coating: *2 lb (1 kg) of couverture chocolate (see recipe on page 61)*

Bring the heavy cream to the boil. Add the tea and leave to infuse for 5 to 10 minutes in the simmering cream. Strain through a sieve. Remove from the heat and slowly add the chocolate, broken into small pieces. Stir with a whisk until the mixture is smooth. Add the vanilla powder. Leave the ganache to stand in a cool place (60°F to 65°F; 15°C to 18°C) for at least 4 hours until it sets. Divide into about 70 pieces with a disk cutter or into balls, if easier. Keep in a cool place so that they become firm. Prepare the couverture chocolate (see recipe on page 61). Dip the ganache balls in the couverture chocolate one at time. Then remove them with a chocolate fork (an ordinary fork will do). Place carefully on greaseproof paper and leave until cold. If you have decided to make disks (*palets*), trace decorative shapes in the coating with a chocolate fork as it begins to set.

THE CANNELLA

Makes 70

For the ganache: *I cup (250 g) of heavy cream, I tsp (5 g) of grated cinnamon, 9 oz (250 g) of chocolate (at least 72 percent cocoa), pinch of vanilla powder*
For the coating: *2 lb (I kg) of couverture chocolate (see recipe on page 61)*

Bring the cream to the boil. Add the grated cinnamon and leave to infuse for 5 to 10 minutes in the simmering cream. Strain through a sieve. Remove from the heat and slowly add the chocolate, broken into small pieces. Stir the mixture with a whisk until it is smooth. Add the pinch of vanilla powder. Leave the ganache to stand in a cool place (60°F to 65°F; 15°C to 18°C) for at least 4 hours until it sets. Divide into about 70 balls. Keep in a cool place so that they become firm. Prepare the couverture chocolate (see recipe on page 61). Dip the ganache balls in the couverture chocolate one at time. Then remove them with a chocolate fork (an ordinary fork will do). Place carefully on greaseproof paper and leave until cold.

THE MARCO POLO

Makes 70

For the ganache: *I cup (250 g) of heavy cream, 9 oz (250 g) of chocolate (at least 72 percent cocoa), $\frac{1}{8}$ to $\frac{1}{4}$ lb (50 to 100 g) (according to taste) of very finely chopped candied ginger, pinch of vanilla*
For the coating: *2 lb 6 oz (1.2 kg) of couverture chocolate (see recipe on page 61)*

Bring the cream to the boil. Remove from the heat and slowly add the chocolate, broken into small pieces. Stir the mixture with a whisk until smooth. Add the ginger and the pinch of vanilla powder. Stir well to ensure the ingredients are evenly distributed. Leave the ganache to stand in a cool place (60°F to 65°F; 15°C to 18°C) for at least 4 hours until it sets. Divide into about 70 balls. Keep in a cool place so that they become firm. Prepare the couverture chocolate (see recipe on page 61). Dip the ganache balls in the couverture chocolate one at time. Then remove them with a chocolate fork (an ordinary fork will do). Place carefully on greaseproof paper and leave until cold.

The Cannella.

THE MAQUIS

Makes 70

For the ganache: *1 cup (250g) heavy cream, 9 oz (250 g) of chocolate (at least 72 percent cocoa), 4 to 5 oz (100 to 150 g) (according to taste) of very finely chopped candied orange peel, 1 spoonful of mandarin liqueur, pinch of vanilla powder*
For the coating: *2 lb 6 oz (1.2 kg) of coating chocolate (see recipe on page 61)*

Bring the cream to the boil. Remove from the heat and slowly add the chocolate, broken into small pieces. Stir the mixture with a whisk until smooth. Add the candied orange peel, the liqueur, and a pinch of vanilla powder. Stir well to ensure the ingredients are evenly distributed. Leave the ganache to stand in a cool place (60°F to 65°F; 15°C to 18°C) for at least 4 hours until it sets. Divide into about 70 balls. Keep in a cool place so that they become firm. Prepare the coating chocolate (see recipe on page 61). Dip the ganache balls in the coating chocolate one at time. Then remove them with a chocolate fork (an ordinary fork will do). Place carefully on greaseproof paper and leave until cold.

THE LINNÉ (LINNAEUS)

Makes 70

For the ganache: *1 cup (250 g) of heavy cream, ½ stick (50 g) of butter, 9 oz (250 g) of chocolate (at least 72 percent cocoa), 2 oz (50 g) of cocoa nibs (roasted, crushed beans), pinch of vanilla powder*
For the coating: *2 lb 6 oz (1.2 kg) of coating chocolate (see recipe on page 61)*

Bring the cream to the boil with the butter. Remove from the heat and slowly add the chocolate, broken into small pieces. Stir the mixture with a whisk until smooth. Add the cocoa nibs and pinch of vanilla powder. Stir well to ensure the ingredients are evenly distributed. Leave the ganache to stand in a cool place (60°F to 65°F; 15°C to 18°C) for at least 4 hours until it sets. Divide into about 70 pieces and shape into balls. Keep in a cool place so that they become firm. Prepare the coating chocolate (see recipe on page 61). Dip the ganache balls in the coating chocolate one at time. Then remove them with a chocolate fork (an ordinary fork will do). Place carefully on greaseproof paper and leave until cold.

Tip: only add the nibs once the ganache is thoroughly blended, then mix well to ensure they are evenly distributed.

The Linné. Named after the distinguished botanist Linnaeus, who gave the cocoa tree its scientific name, Theobroma: drink of the gods.

RASPBERRY PALETS

Makes 70

For the ganache: *½ cup (150 g) of heavy cream, ¼ stick (25 g) of butter, 9 oz (250 g) of chocolate (at least 72 percent cocoa), 2½ oz (75 g) of raspberry pulp, 1 tbsp of raspberry liqueur, pinch of vanilla powder*
For the coating: *2 lb (1 kg) of couverture chocolate (see recipe on page 61)*

Bring the cream to the boil with the butter. Remove from the heat and slowly add the chocolate, broken into small pieces. Stir the mixture with a whisk until smooth. Add the raspberry pulp, liqueur, and pinch of vanilla powder. Stir well to ensure the ingredients are evenly distributed. Leave the ganache to stand in a cool place (60°F to 65°F; 15°C to 18°C) for at least 4 hours until it sets. Divide into about 70 pieces using a circular cutter, or shape into balls if easier. Keep in a cool place so that they become firm. Prepare the couverture chocolate (see recipe on page 61). Dip the ganache balls in the couverture chocolate one at time. Then remove them with a chocolate fork (an ordinary fork will do). Place carefully on greaseproof paper and leave until cold. If you have decided to make *palets*, trace decorative shapes in the coating as it begins to set using a chocolate fork.

The Royal.

THE ROYAL

Makes 70

For the ganache: *1 scant cup (200 g) of heavy cream, ½ stick (50 g) of butter, 9 oz (250 g) of chocolate (at least 72 percent cocoa), pinch of vanilla powder*
For the coating: *2 lb (1 kg) of couverture chocolate (see recipe on page 61)*

Bring the cream to the boil with the butter. Remove from the heat and slowly add the chocolate, broken into small pieces. Stir the mixture with a whisk until smooth. Add the pinch of vanilla powder. Stir well to ensure the ingredients are evenly distributed. Leave the ganache to stand in a cool place (60°F to 65°F; 15°C to 18°C) for at least 4 hours until it sets. Divide into about 70 pieces and shape into balls. Keep in a cool place so that they become firm. Prepare the couverture chocolate (see recipe on page 61). Dip the ganache balls in the couverture chocolate one at time. Then remove them with a chocolate fork (an ordinary fork will do). Place carefully on greaseproof paper and leave until cold.

THE FLEUR DE LYS

Makes 70

For the ganache: *1 cup (250 g) of heavy cream, ¼ stick (25 g) of butter, 9 oz (250 g) of chocolate (at least 72 percent cocoa), 1½ tbsp (25 g) of liquid caramel, pinch of vanilla powder*
For the coating: *1 lb (500 g) of couverture chocolate (see recipe on page 61)*

Bring the cream to the boil with the butter. Remove from the heat and slowly add the chocolate broken into small pieces. Stir the mixture with a whisk until smooth. Add the liquid caramel and pinch of vanilla powder. Stir well to ensure the ingredients are evenly distributed. Leave the ganache to stand in a cool place (60°F to 65°F; 15°C to 18°C) for at least 4 hours until it sets. Divide into about 70 pieces and shape into balls. Keep in a cool place so that they become firm. Prepare the couverture chocolate (see recipe on page 61). Dip the ganache balls in the coating chocolate one at time. Then remove them with a chocolate fork (an ordinary fork will do). Place carefully on greaseproof paper and leave until cold.

THE INCROYABLE

Makes 70

For the ganache: *1 scant cup (200 g) of heavy cream, ½ lb (200 g) of chocolate (at least 72 percent cocoa), pinch of vanilla powder, ½ lb (200 g) of nougatine (½ cup (100 g) of cane sugar, 1 cup (100 g) of roughly chopped, blanched almonds)*
For the coating: *2 lb 6 oz (1.2 kg) of couverture chocolate (see recipe on page 61)*

Bring the cream to the boil. Remove from the heat and slowly add the chocolate, broken into small pieces. Stir the mixture with a whisk until smooth. Add the pinch of vanilla powder. Stir well to ensure the ingredients are evenly distributed. Leave the ganache to stand in a cool place (60°F to 65°F; 15°C to 18°C) for at least 4 hours until it sets. Toast the almonds on a baking tray in an oven at 480°F (250°C; mark 8/9). Moisten the sugar and place on a low heat. As soon as it begins to turn brown, add the toasted almonds. Spread the mixture on a cold baking sheet or tray and once it has set, crush before adding to the ganache mixture. Divide into about 70 pieces and shape into balls. Keep in a cool place so that they become firm. Prepare the coating chocolate (see recipe on page 61). Dip the ganache balls in the couverture chocolate one at time. Then remove them with a chocolate fork (an ordinary fork will do). Place carefully on greaseproof paper and leave until cold.

The Fleur de Lys.

THE SAINTS-PÈRES

Makes 70

For the praline: *1 cup (150 g) of whole, blanched almonds, ¾ cup (100 g) of whole hazelnuts, 1 cup (250 g) of cane sugar, 5 oz (150 g) of couverture chocolate (see recipe on page 61)*
For the coating: *3 lb 1 oz (1.450 kg) of couverture chocolate (see recipe on page 61)*

Preheat the oven to 480°F (250°C; mark 8/9). Toast the whole, blanched almonds on a baking tray. Separately toast the hazelnuts. Remove the skin from the hazelnuts by rubbing them between your hands as soon as they are cool enough. Moisten the sugar and place in a pan on a low heat, stirring all the time. When it begins to take color, remove immediately from the heat and add the nuts to the pan. Pour the mixture in a thin layer onto a lightly oiled, cold baking tray. Once the mixture has set, break it into small pieces and grind to a paste in a blender. Prepare 3 lb 6 oz (1.6 kg) of couverture chocolate (see the recipe on page 61). Take 5 oz (150 g) and set the rest aside. Add the chocolate to the praline paste, stirring well with a spatula to ensure all the ingredients are evenly distributed. Leave the mixture to rest. Once firm, divide into 70 pieces and shape into balls. Keep these in a cool place. Dip the balls in the couverture chocolate one at time. Remove them with a chocolate fork (an ordinary fork will do), place carefully on greaseproof paper, and leave until cold.

Fine champagne truffles.

FINE CHAMPAGNE TRUFFLES

Makes 70

For the ganache: *1 cup (250 g) of light cream, 9 oz (250 g) of chocolate (at least 72 percent cocoa), 1 tbsp (10 cl) of fine champagne (or another alcohol of your choice), pinch of vanilla*
For the coating: *2 lb 2 oz (1 kg) of couverture chocolate (see recipe on page 61), 1 lb 2 oz (500 g) of cocoa powder*

Bring the cream to the boil. Remove from the heat and slowly add the chocolate broken into small pieces, carefully stirring the mixture with a fork. Add the champagne and the vanilla. Stir until smooth. Stand the ganache in a cool place (60°F to 65°F; 15°C to 18°C) for at least 4 hours, and if possible for a whole day. Take the ganache and, if it is too hard, reheat it slightly. Divide into about 70 pieces, roll into balls by hand, and keep in a cool place. Prepare the couverture chocolate (see recipe on page 61). Make a mound of the cocoa powder. Dip the balls one at a time into the couverture chocolate. Then place them carefully in the cocoa and roll them with a chocolate fork until coated in powder. Stir the couverture chocolate regularly with a spatula. As soon as it becomes too thick check the temperature and, if necessary, reheat it slightly on a low heat, stirring all the time until it returns to 99°F (37°C). When all the balls have been dipped and rolled, place them carefully, 6 at a time, in a sieve and shake gently to remove any excess cocoa. Keep the truffles in a cool place until ready to serve.

PRALINE BALLS

Makes 80

For the praline: *1¹/₃ cup (150 g) of blanched almonds, ¾ cup (100 g) of hazelnuts, 1 cup (250 g) of cane sugar, 5 oz (150 g) of couverture chocolate*
For the coating: *2½ lb (1.3 kg) of couverture chocolate (see recipe on page 61)*

Preheat the oven to 480°F (250°C; mark 8/9). Toast the whole, blanched almonds on a baking tray. Separately toast the hazelnuts. Remove the skin from the hazelnuts by rubbing them between your hands as soon as they are cool enough. Moisten the sugar and place in a pan on a low heat, stirring all the time. When it begins to take color, remove immediately from the heat and add the nuts to the pan. Pour the mixture in a thin layer onto a lightly oiled, cold baking tray. Once the mixture has set, break it into small pieces and grind to a paste in a blender. Prepare 3 lb 1 oz (1.450 kg) of couverture chocolate (see the recipe on page 61). Take 5 oz (150 g) and set the rest aside. Add the chocolate to the praline paste, stirring well with a spatula to ensure all the ingredients are evenly distributed. Leave the mixture to rest. Once firm, divide into 80 pieces and roll by hand into balls. Keep these in a cool place. Dip the balls in the couverture chocolate one at time and place them carefully on greaseproof paper. Stir the couverture chocolate regularly with a spatula. As soon as it becomes too thick check the temperature and, if necessary, reheat it slightly over a very low heat, stirring all the time until it returns to 99°F (37°C). Keep the balls in a cool place until ready to serve.

CHOCOLATE DESSERTS

FONDANT
Prepare a day in advance

Serves 8
Preparation: 30 minutes
Cooking time: 1 hour

Ingredients: *1 cup (250 g) of sugar, 9 oz (250 g) of chocolate (70 percent cocoa), 2 sticks (250 g) of butter (plus some to grease the tin), ¾ cup (75 g) of flour, 3 eggs, grated chocolate and icing sugar to dust*

In a medium-sized pan, boil ½ a glass of water with the sugar. Add the chocolate broken into small pieces, along with the butter and stir over a low heat until the mixture is smooth. In a bowl, mix together the flower and one whole egg. Then add the remaining two eggs one at a time. Remove the chocolate mixture from the heat and pour the mixture in the bowl onto the chocolate mix. Stir vigorously. Butter an 8 in. (20 cm) cake tin and pour in the mixture. Place the tin in a container of warm water and bake in a medium oven at 390°F (200°C; mark 6/7) for 1 hour. Remove from the oven and leave to cool until the following day. Garnish with the grated chocolate and dust with icing sugar. Delicious served with a light vanilla or coffee-flavored custard.

CHOCOLATE AND COFFEE CHARLOTTE

Prepare a day in advance

Serves 6
Preparation: 45 minutes
Cooking time: 10 minutes
Refrigeration: overnight

Ingredients: *4½ oz (125 g) of chocolate (70 percent cocoa), ½ stick (50 g) of butter (plus some to grease the tin), 4 eggs, 30 spoon cookies, 1 glass of very strong, sweetened, black coffee, grated or granulated chocolate for decoration*

Break the chocolate into pieces, add the butter, and melt together in a bain-marie. Once the mixture is smooth and creamy, add the egg yolks. Continue to stir (still in the bain-marie). Remove from the heat and add the stiffly beaten egg whites. Put in a cool place and set aside a little of the mousse for decoration. Line the bottom and sides of a buttered cake tin with spoon cookies (curved side against the tin). Soak the remaining biscuits in the coffee. Fill the tin with alternate layers of chocolate mousse and coffee-flavored cookies. Leave to rest in the refrigerator overnight. Turn out onto a long dish, spread the mousse you set aside for decoration on top of the dessert, and sprinkle with grated or granulated chocolate. Delicious served with a light vanilla custard.

CHOCOLATE PROFITEROLES

Serves 6
Preparation: 20 minutes
Resting time: 30 minutes
Cooking time: 40 minutes

Ingredients: *½ lb (200 g) of fondant chocolate (72 percent cocoa), ¾ cup (20 cl) of crème fraîche, 2 cups (500 g) of Chantilly cream or vanilla ice cream* **For the choux pastry:** *½ pint (25 cl) of water, ½ stick (75 g) of butter, a pinch of salt, 1 tbsp of sugar, ½ cup (125 g) of flour, 3 eggs*

Begin with the choux pastry. Put ½ pint (25 cl) of water into a pan with the diced butter, salt, and sugar. Bring to the boil. Add all the flour at once stirring vigorously until the mixture forms into a soft ball of paste that leaves the sides of the pan clean. Remove from the heat. Add the eggs one at a time, stirring to blend in each egg before adding the next. Leave to rest for 30 minutes. Divide into small balls and place on a baking tray. Bake in the oven at 355°F (180°C; mark 6) for approximately 30 minutes. Leave to cool. Now melt the chocolate in a bain-marie. Add the crème fraîche. When the pastry balls are cool, split them open and fill with Chantilly cream or vanilla ice cream. Arrange in a pyramid and pour the hot chocolate over the top. Serve warm or cold.

GRANDMA'S CHOCOLATE CREAM DESSERT

Serves 6
Preparation: 20 minutes
Cooking time: 15 minutes

Ingredients: *½ lb (200 g) of dark chocolate (70 percent cocoa), 1 quart (1 liter) of full cream milk, 5 eggs*

Break the chocolate into pieces in a pan and melt over water on a very low heat. Once the mixture is smooth, add the milk and bring to the boil, whisking all the time. Separate the whites from the yolks. Beat the yolks in a bowl and gradually add the warm chocolate milk. Thicken the mixture in a bain-marie, stirring gently until it returns to the boil. Pour the cream dessert into small, individual ramekins and leave to rest in the refrigerator.

CHOCOLATE MOUSSE

Serves 6
Preparation: 20 minutes
Cooking time: 5 minutes
Refrigeration: 2 hours

Ingredients: *4 eggs, 4 tbsp of sugar, ¼ lb (100 g) of dark chocolate (70 percent cocoa), 1 stick (100 g) of butter, 1 tbsp of very strong coffee*

Beat the egg yolks with the sugar until pale. Soften the chocolate in a bain-marie. Add the egg and sugar mixture, and stir. Gradually add the butter, blending as you go to form an even mixture. Add coffee to flavor (optional). Beat the egg whites until very stiff. Add them gently to the mixture. Leave to stand for 2 hours in a cool place before serving.

Serves 6
Preparation: 25 minutes
Cooking time: 30 minutes

Ingredients: *5 oz (150 g) of dark chocolate (70 percent cocoa), 1 ¾ cup (50 cl) of full cream milk, 5 eggs, ¼ cup (30 g) of flour, 2 tbsp, firmly packed (30 g) of sugar*

Preheat the oven to 390°F (200°C; mark 6/7). Melt the chocolate in a pan on a very low heat with just a little water. Add the milk and bring to the boil, stirring continuously. Set aside. Separate the eggs. In a bowl, beat the yolks. Gradually add these to the chocolate mixture, stirring with a spatula. Blend the flour and sugar with a little of the remaining milk. Add to the mixture, stirring vigorously. Beat the egg whites until very stiff. Add them carefully to the mixture. Pour into a soufflé mold. Place in the oven and cook for 20 minutes without opening the oven door. Serve immediately!

CHOCOLATE PUDDING
Prepare a day in advance

Serves 6
Preparation: 30 minutes
Cooking time: 5 minutes
Refrigeration: overnight

Ingredients: *5 oz (150 g) of chocolate (70 percent cocoa), water, 4 eggs, ⅓ cup (80 g) of sugar, ½ stick (60 g) of butter, 4½ oz (125 g) of dry cookies*

Break the chocolate into pieces in a pan and melt with just a little water over a low heat. Separate the eggs and set the whites aside. Stir the yolks and sugar into the mixture with a spatula. Beat the egg whites until stiff. Add to the mixture. Add the softened butter. Line a dish with the cookies and pour in the mixture. Cover with another layer of cookies. Leave to rest overnight in a cool place.

CHOCOLATE ICE CREAM

Serves 4

Preparation: 15 minutes

Cooking time: 10 minutes

Ingredients: *2 cups (500 ml) of milk, 6 egg yolks, 1 cup (200 g) of sugar, ¾ cup (100 g) of unsweetened cocoa, ⅔ pint (300 ml) of liquid crème fraîche*

Bring the milk to the boil in a pan. In a bowl, beat the egg yolks with ½ cup (100 g) of sugar until pale. Add the cocoa and mix thoroughly. Pour the milk in slowly, stirring all the time until the mixture is runny. Return to a low heat to thicken but do not allow to boil. Leave to cool. Whip the crème fraîche and the rest of the sugar then add to the mixture. Churn until firm. Enjoy!

CONCLUSION

Chocolate is a source of pleasure and shared enjoyment, offering a wealth of rich aromas that are the delight of young and old alike across the world. Whether consumed in the form of chocolate candies such as *rochers* or *palets*, or as simple chocolate bars, or transformed into a charlotte, a fondant, a cake, or an ice cream, chocolate loses nothing of its flavor or sensual delight.

Auguste Gallais ends his *Cocoa Monograph* by describing the intense pleasures that chocolate imparts: "Those fortunate enough," he writes, "to have been endowed by nature with exceptional organs of taste, know what sweet satisfaction is brought to their palate by the foamy, flavorsome liquor that is a well-made cup of chocolate; they recall with deep pleasure the happy harmony that comes from the union of vanilla and cocoa, and bless the day that industrial progress made chocolate a portable food whose benefits can be enjoyed at any time we wish."

The true magic of chocolate lies precisely in its capacity to generate this passion and adoration in those who sample it.